Robot M

Written by Tony Hyland

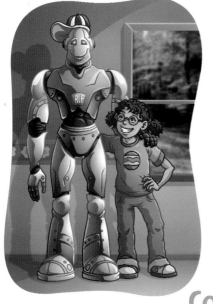

Contents

Rigby.

Chapter Snapshots

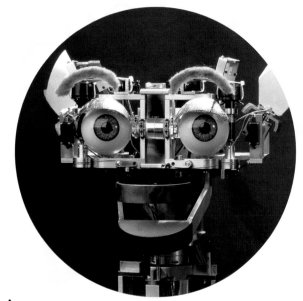

Introduction PAGE 4

What is a robot? Are all machines robots? Find out what makes a robot.

1 Hard at Work PAGE 6

Robots can work all day and all night. It's lucky they don't get bored.

2 Danger! Danger!
PAGE 12

Robots work in some of the most dangerous places in the world—or away from it!

**"Most robots are hard workers,
but some robots are fun …"**

Introduction

Would you like your own robot? What would your robot do? Would it look like a person?

What Is a Robot?

Cars and airplanes are machines that can move around, but they are not robots. A computer can do clever things, but it is not a robot.

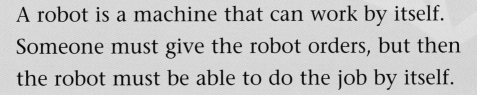

A robot is a machine that can work by itself.
Someone must give the robot orders, but then
the robot must be able to do the job by itself.

Some robots look a bit like a human. These are
called humanoid robots. Other robots have
wheels or tracks like a tank.

1 Hard at Work

This robot works in a factory.

Most robots work in factories. They do hard or boring jobs.

Not many robots look like humans. Robots are made in the best shape to do their job. In a factory, a robot may look like a long arm, with an elbow and a wrist.

Would You Get Bored?

Robots can keep on doing the same job, over and over. Imagine doing one small job, over and over, every day. Would you get bored? Robots are good at these jobs because they don't get bored.

Car factories have many one-armed robots in rows. Each robot does one job. One will drill holes. Another robot will weld parts together. Another robot sprays paint.

This car factory has many robots working on cars.

A robot needs to sense where to move and what to do. It must be able to tell that it is in the right place and doing the right thing. It's not good if a robot welder is welding the wrong car part.

Control Your Robot

It's not easy to tell a robot what to do. You must tell it every step.

Try this with a friend. Pretend your friend is a robot. Get your friend to pick something up from a table. BUT—you can only use these robot commands:

Forward   *Arm up*
Back   *Arm down*
Turn right   *Open fingers*
Turn left   *Close fingers*

How did you do? Do you need any more commands?

In this factory, robot vehicles move around. They carry car parts. These robots can tell when it is time to get more parts. They know where to go because people have told them.

Don't Try This at Home!

Robots can make very small, careful movements. Some robots can operate on people! The robots can do some things that are difficult for a doctor to do. However, a doctor must still be in control of a surgical robot.

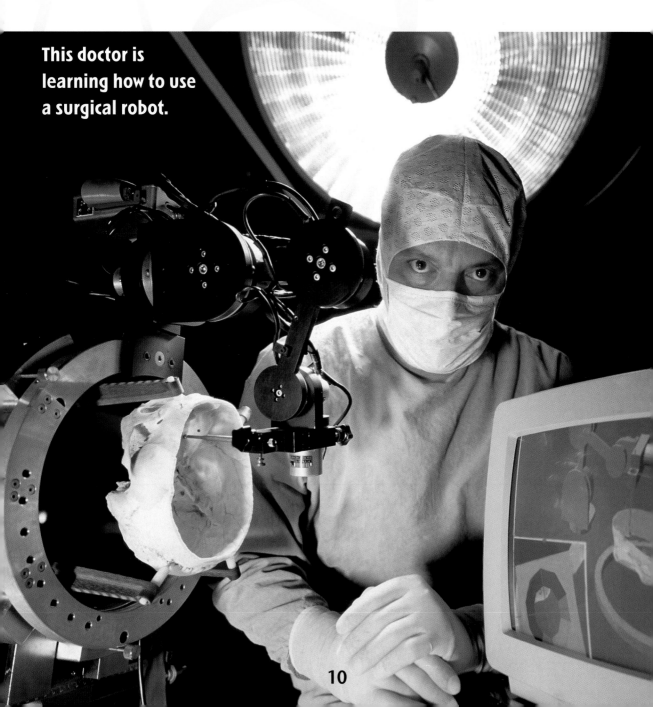

This doctor is learning how to use a surgical robot.

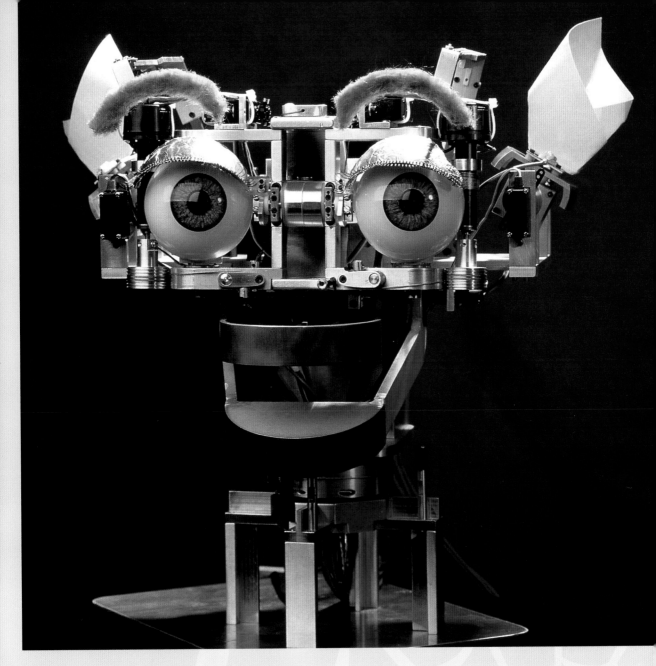

The Friendly Robot

Meet Kismet! If you are friendly, Kismet will be friendly to you. Kismet has eyes, eyebrows, and a mouth with lips. It is the first robot that can show expressions. Kismet can show sadness, happiness, fear, anger, and surprise. These expressions are easy for us humans but very hard for a robot.

2 Danger! Danger!

Sometimes robots do dangerous jobs.

A volcano is a place that is too dangerous for humans. Yet, this robot can travel deep into a live volcano. It picks up rocks. It also checks the heat and the gases in the volcano.

Keeping Safe

Robots can help with many other dangerous jobs. If the police find a suspicious package, they can send a crawler robot to check it.

The crawler robot has a video camera so that the police can look at the suspicious package safely. The robot can make sure the package is safe by using the tools on its long arm.

A Robot on Mars

Sojourner is the name of this robot. In 1997, it was the first robot on Mars! It has six wheels and is as big as a dog. It rolls around slowly, exploring the planet of Mars.

Sojourner took photos and did tests on Mars. Then it sent the information back to Earth.

Underwater Robots

Some robots travel deep under the sea, where humans cannot go. They have lights, a video camera, and long arms with grabbers to pick up interesting things from the seabed.

What Might Underwater Robots See?

It is dark and cold at the bottom of the sea. Strange creatures live there, such as giant squid and glowing fish. The anglerfish waves a light in front of its mouth. When little creatures come along to look at the light—SNAP! —the anglerfish eats them.

Mars Rover 2004

This robot is the Mars Rover of 2004. There are plans for two of these robots to land on the planet Mars. Scientists will use these robots to explore and learn about Mars. Each Mars Rover weighs about 400 pounds. That's a pretty heavy robot!

Solar panels provide energy.

Six wide wheels help the Rover on rough ground.

Video camera
sends TV pictures
to Earth.

Tools pick up rocks and dust
from the ground.

3 Dreaming of Robots

In the 13th century, people dreamed of what life would be like with robots. They drew pictures and called these robots automatons, self-operating machines. Back then they did not have the technology to build their automatons. Slowly, things changed.

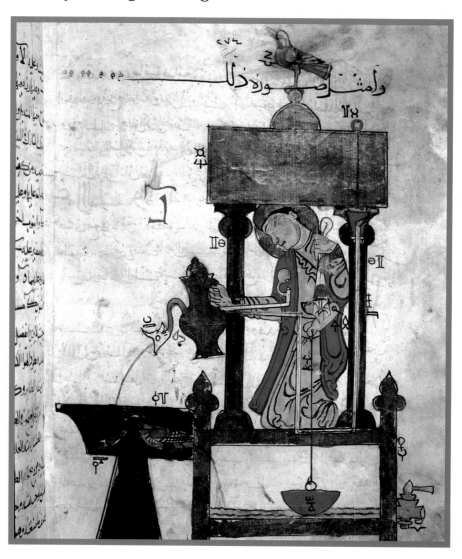

In the late 18th century, many people began experimenting with self-operating machines. The machines became more and more lifelike, like this clockwork instrument-playing robot built in 1785.

People often dream of robots
doing their household chores.

Someday robots might be
able to iron our clothes
and cook our food.

Can you think of a chore
you would like a robot to
do for you?

4 Robot Fun

Most robots are hard working, but some robots are fun to play with.

Robots, or Real Pets?

Would you rather have a robot pet or a real pet?

Real pets need food and shelter. You have to clean up after real pets. Real pets need love. You can't switch off a real pet.

Would you like a real pet or a robot? Why?

Can a Robot Play Soccer?

These robots can.

Each team has a group of robots. The robots move around on a table and try to find the ball. When they find it, they kick the ball toward their goal. A robot goalkeeper tries to stop the ball.

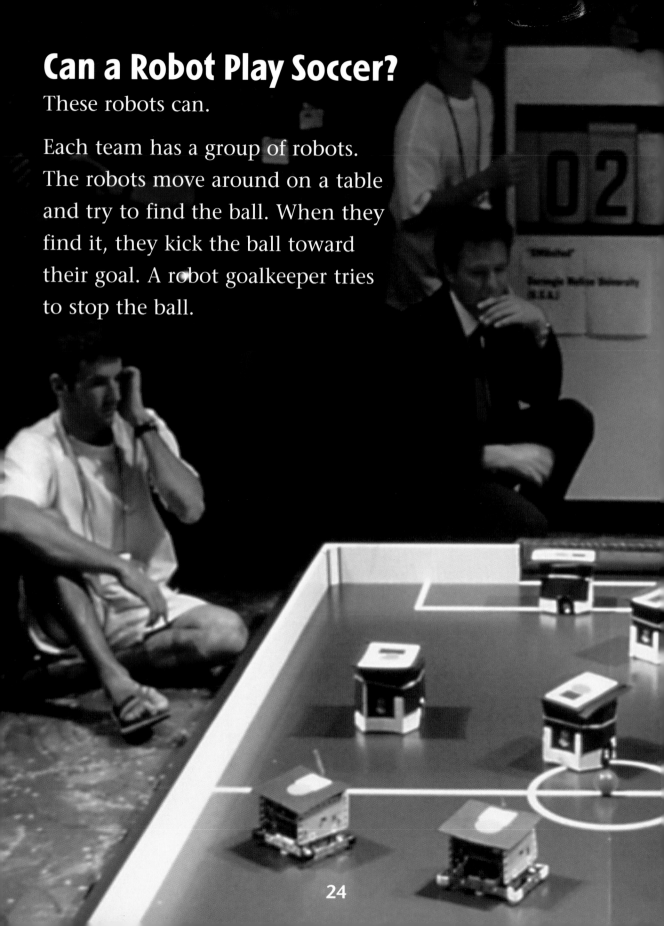

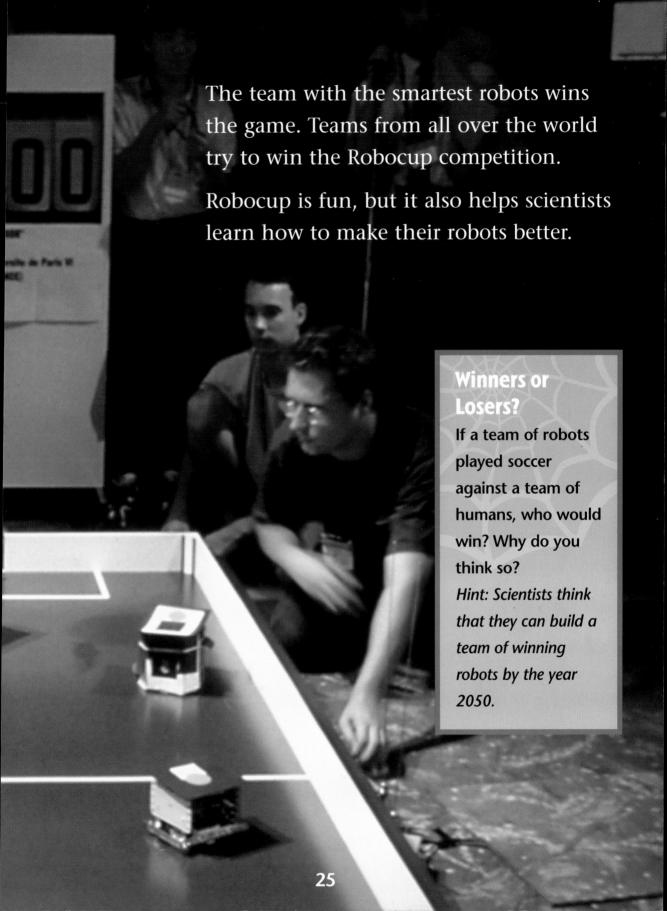

The team with the smartest robots wins the game. Teams from all over the world try to win the Robocup competition.

Robocup is fun, but it also helps scientists learn how to make their robots better.

Winners or Losers?

If a team of robots played soccer against a team of humans, who would win? Why do you think so?

Hint: Scientists think that they can build a team of winning robots by the year 2050.

5 Future Robots

What will robots be like in the future? No one knows for sure, but we can guess.

People will think of new ways to use robots.

Will you have a robot at home? It probably won't look like a human. This vacuum cleaner is a robot. It rolls around the house, cleaning the floor. But it can't wash the dishes or make the beds.

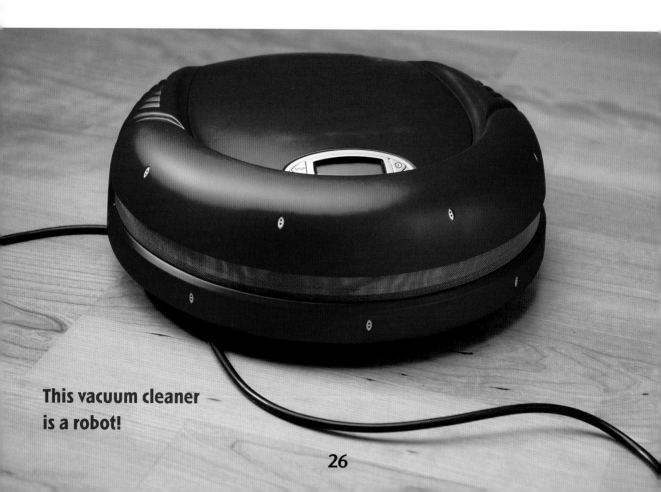

This vacuum cleaner is a robot!

Micro-robots

In the future, some robots could be very small. Tiny robot helicopters could fly around farms, killing insect pests.

What about a tiny robot window cleaner? Just leave it on the window. It will clean the window and you won't even notice it!

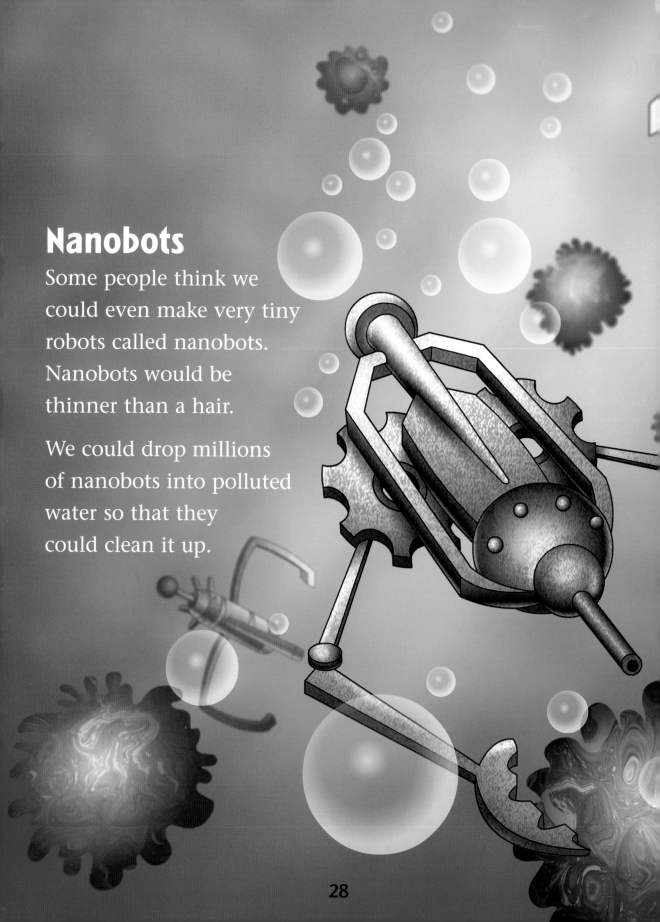

Nanobots

Some people think we could even make very tiny robots called nanobots. Nanobots would be thinner than a hair.

We could drop millions of nanobots into polluted water so that they could clean it up.

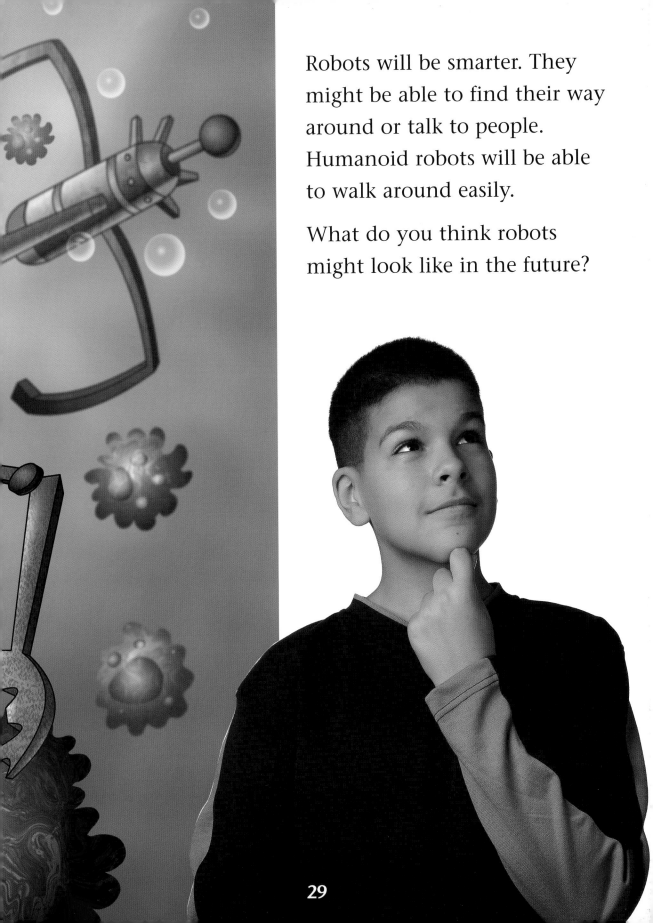

Robots will be smarter. They might be able to find their way around or talk to people. Humanoid robots will be able to walk around easily.

What do you think robots might look like in the future?

Do you think that you will ever see
an advertisement like this?

SPECIAL–
This Week Only

Are you lonely? Do you need a friend?
Would you like someone to help you
with your homework?
You need Robo-friend!

Robo-friend:

- always friendly
- never argues
- plays all of your favorite outdoor games
  —basketball, baseball, soccer
- great sense of humor
- knows thousands of jokes
- can help with your homework

Robo-friend—*always there when
you need a friend*

Index

Bookweb Links

Key to Bookweb Fact Boxes

- ■ Arts
- ■ Health
- ■ Science
- ■ Social Studies
- ■ Technology

Read more Grade 3 books in Bookweb and Bookweb Plus about how technology is changing the way we live and work:

What's the Problem? — Nonfiction

Home Technology — Nonfiction

The Butcher, the Baker ... — Nonfiction

At the Movies — Nonfiction

The Streetsweeper — Fiction

A Painter Called Vincent — Fiction